Who Stole My Blanket?

Paulette,
May God cover you
with his blanket of
protection all your days!
Jote
6-16-14

6 Easy Steps to Rebuild Your Life after an Income Loss

C. Joyce Farrar-Rosemon

WINNER AT LIFE PUBLISHERS
ATLANTA, GEORGIA

ISBN: 0985626208
ISBN: 978-0-9856262-0-4

Printed in the United States of America

WINNER AT LIFE PUBLISHERS
ATLANTA, GEORGIA 30281
WWW.WOMENSEMPOWERMENTSEMINARS.COM
404-202-8776

DISCLAIMER

All of the information in this book contains the views and opinions of the author, and the views and opinions of the author can change. This is a GUIDE ONLY and the information should be used with DISCRETION, wisdom, and at your own risk. The author and You Can Be A Winner At Life! © disclaim any liability for personal and business loss caused by the use of information in this book.

CONTENTS

ACKNOWLEDGEMENTS

I must give honor to whom honor is due--three outstanding men who have challenged me to shoot for the stars. First, I would be remiss not to give thanks posthumously, to Reverend Dr. Martin Luther King Jr. His writings have inspired me to write, achieve, and serve mankind. His sacrificial life has left an indelible mark on how I choose to live my life. This quote of his in particular has been extremely motivating: "Whatever your life's work is, do it well. A man should do his job so well that the living, the dead, and the unborn could do it no better."

Secondly, honorable mention is also given to the late President John F. Kennedy Jr. His challenge to all Americans and to me was to: "Ask not what your country can do for you, but ask what you can do for your country."

And lastly, a recent quote from President Barack Obama echoes and reframes the words of the late great former president. In President Obama's challenge to Americans he stated the following: "Focusing your life solely on making a buck shows a certain poverty of ambition. It asks too little of yourself. Because it's only when you hitch your wagon to something larger than yourself that you realize your true potential."

All three of these great men shared a spirit of altruism. If we could all live our lives similarly, we would be the change that leaves an enduring mark that generations from now our descendants will look back and say that we truly were the enlightened ones, because like the military, we left no man or woman behind!

INTRODUCTION

"Oh the good old days have passed" is a familiar lament. Many will tell their offspring that there was a time during the late 20th-early 21st century when the economy was really booming. Homes were appreciating exponentially and houses were selling almost before you could put a real estate sign in the ground. Advertisements coaxed buyers into signing on the dotted line so that they could get a piece of prosperity now. There was no need to worry about what would happen when the loan adjusted to a higher rate, because you could always sell it and make a profit.

Yes, this is what many unscrupulous loan officers, appraisers, and real estate agents told unsuspecting and uninformed buyers. Many buyers listened and heard what they wanted to hear. Their ears and their eyes told them that their future home with a whirlpool tub, granite countertops, and stainless steel appliances would offer them security and an excellent investment that would appreciate within a short period of time.

But, unfortunately the economy regurgitated these false truths and house by house, like *Linus, from the Charlie Brown* (http://youtu.be/E7ID_E-SYbQ) cartoon series, many homeowners' security blankets were stolen from under them.[1] Yes, in the first decade of the 21st century we are left with a global

---

1 TickleMeCthulhu, *linus in withdrawals*. YouTube. December 1, 2010.

economic mess that many say parallels The Great Depression.

But, here is the good news, the same way we survived The Great Depression, we will overcome this 21st century recession! *So, don't panic if you feel that someone has stolen your security blanket.* Don't despair if you have been fired, downsized, lost your job, your retirement, stocks, bonds, pension, your house, spouse, or have become a victim of a natural disaster. Yes, sadly, sometimes when the money gets funny, so-called friends, love ones, employers, and associates will abandon or fire you.

Who am I to give advice, you might ask? Well, I've been around the block a few times. I have not only survived, but I have thrived after living in a dysfunctional family. *I've overcome poverty, abuse, loneliness, depression, job loss, a stillbirth and two miscarriages.* I've learned how to "use what you got" (as my mom would say) to come out on top. In '92 I opened a real estate company with my husband's help in my 7th month of pregnancy with only $10.00 in the operating account. That $10.00 subsequently blossomed into a six-figure income.

I've gone from making six figures--to no figures--having survived unemployment and various low paying jobs after the real estate debacle that began in 2007. Finally, after going back to school-- and filling out close to 400 applications over a two year period-- I landed a job as a Certified Educator at the age of 57.

Inside these pages I have *6 easy steps to get you back on your road to economic recovery!* What I have learned is being passed on to you now so that you can experience your own success and economic revival. Stick to these 6 steps I've outlined in the following pages. Trust the process, and *I guarantee* that like a seed planted and watered in good soil with ample light--*you too will come out of your economic crisis on top!* It's in you--trust me. Now read on so that you can make it happen!

P.S. Like a fine aged wine that accompanies an extraordinary meal, this is an interactive book that is best enjoyed by clicking on the hyperlinks that accompany the text. If you bypass them, you will miss the humor, wisdom, and full flavor that this quick read has to offer.

Step 1:

Swallow Your Pride

The thief comes only to steal and kill and to destroy; I have come that they might have life, and have it to the full.

John 10:10 NIV

Okay admit it-- swallow your pride, somehow, some way, someone has stolen your security blanket! Maybe you were hoodwinked, taken advantage of, lied to, cheated, misinformed, passed up for a promotion, or your job was sent overseas,-- "blah, blah, blah"--the list goes on and on! Maybe you are like Linus in the cartoon, *Linus in withdrawal* (http://youtu.be/E7ID_E-SYbQ) and you are walking through life feeling insecure without your security blanket.[2]

In the above video Linus complains to Charlie Brown that since he gave his blanket to Charlie Brown, he can't be without it. He says that his life is like a nightmare, he keeps passing out, and walks around saying, "Woe, woe, woe, is me!" Meanwhile, Charlie Brown is dead tired from studying at the library and has no clue where Linus' blanket is. Linus is distraught and threatens to kick Charlie Brown because his friend has been irresponsible with what Linus calls his "good luck charm". His friend, Snoopy, the useless, hunting dog is of no

---

[2] TickleMeCthulhu, *linus in withdrawals*. YouTube. December 1, 2010.

help either. He runs three times to get water for Linus who keeps passing out, but Snoopy instead drinks it himself each time.

So much for friends as the saying goes. Are you like Linus, walking around saying, woe is me? Like Linus your good luck charm, your security blanket is gone--lost, stolen, or disappeared. The question is--what are you going to do about it now? You can't change the past, but you can change the present. Passing out won't change a thing either. It will not put you back on the road to economic recovery. Naming and blaming someone else won't help as well.

The cause of your lost security blanket can be a health challenge, an educational, political, environmental, economic, physical, or spiritual one. Internally it may be your own low self-esteem. This list is not inclusive. You must fill in the blank for yourself. Did you grow up on the wrong side of the track, suffer neglect or abuse as a child or an adult? Have you lost your adolescent figure, lost your spouse, your job, or are you an empty nester?

Regardless of the cause, it is now time to grow up and take responsibility for your stolen blanket. Some of you are probably saying "ouch" right now because like Linus you loved your blanket dearly and you are going through withdrawal symptoms. Maybe like Linus, it doesn't matter how dirty your blanket got, how old, ragged, or out-dated, you still want that symbol of good luck charm around you. Like a woman with low self-esteem, you may feel it's better to have a piece of a man, rather than no man at all.

Nature has designed us to physically mature from childhood to adulthood. Like it or not, we all will get older. The goal however, is to mature into responsible adults. Like Charlie Brown we must get on with life, busy ourselves with school or a vocational pursuit and leave our security blanket at home. They are good memories of former days, but they belong in the past. They are too cumbersome to take with us on our journey through life.

On this voyage we also have to leave behind useless friends like Snoopy that are enablers. They feed into our dysfunction and don't encourage us to grow. They drink the water, the nourishment for themselves and aren't capable of sharing it with us. We like Charlie Brown, must find a transitional object that will take the place of the tangible security blanket that we hold so dear. This one however, needs to be internalized so that in times of uncertainty it surrounds us with a shroud of comfort unseen by others.

But, before we can utilize this transitional object, we must let go of pride and acknowledge that we need help. We have to stop blaming others and realize that our successes and failures in life are based on cause and effect, not lucky charms. Whatever the cause is, you must first acknowledge that you need help, and then come up with an economic recovery plan. Not a government stimulus plan, *but your own plan.*

The problem with pride is that it interferes with our being able to see life and ourselves clearly. Pride causes us to hold on to our accomplishments, our victories of the past. By definition it means to have *a high or inordinate opinion of one's own dignity, importance, merit, or superiority, whether as cherished in the mind or as displayed in bearing, or conduct.*

Don't get me wrong, it is healthy to have pride in one's accomplishments, but when it interferes with your ability to see and admit that life has changed, it can become a dangerous security blanket. Your accomplishments of the past should be transitional objects that facilitate your ability to overcome present-day challenges and achieve new victories in life.

For example, what good is it to tell a prospective boss that you were the top selling typewriter sales representative and therefore he should give you a job selling the latest top selling electronic gadget? Do you know anything about the Apple iPhone 5 64GB electronic gadget? Can you explain its Wifi and 4G capabilities with unrivalled browsing speed, its ability to make calls and connect to Apple's iTunes software which offers millions of songs, thousands of games, and can access literally 1000's of applications to help you do anything from losing weight to accessing your Facebook account?

The point I am making is that pride should not keep you locked into past successes. If the job has been outsourced, why spend needless hours harping on the inequities of the government and politicians who favor business over the common man or woman? Right now you need a job and if you have a family, they want you to provide food on the table and a roof over their head today! Work on getting a job as your top priority and then work on changing the system.

Let go of your pride, go back to school, seek additional training, and stay current. Does your look need to be updated? Do you need your teeth fixed? Look in the mirror, if you look like a couch potato, turn off the TV, walk around the neighborhood, and get some exercise, so that you can lose some weight, and stay healthy. When you are finished exercising, eat some fruits and vegetables and read a book on current trends and the latest inventions. Not about celebrities, but about the latest technological devices, creative ideas that have made people money, *and can make you money*!

Meditate and ask God (or creative intelligence) for witty inventions. Proverbs 8:12 declares, "I wisdom dwell with prudence, and find out knowledge of witty inventions." This advice worked for Madame C.J. Walker, who was uneducated, born in poverty, the child of ex-slaves, suffered abuse and later became the first female millionaire back in the early 1900s, and she just so happened to be African American.

Ms. Walker's million dollar invention came to her in a dream during a time she had faced so many catastrophes that her hair began to fall out. 'One night, I had a dream,' she recounted. 'A man appeared to me and told me what to mix up for my hair. Some of the remedy was grown in Africa, but I sent for it, put it on my scalp, and in a few weeks, my hair was coming in faster than it had ever fallen out.'[3]

---

3 Sullivan, Otha Richard. *African American Women Scientists and Inventors.* (New York: Wiley, 2002), p. 27

At The National Negro Business League Convention in July 1912, a portion of her speech was as follows, "I am a woman who came from the cotton fields of the South. I was promoted to the washtub. From there I was promoted to the cook kitchen. And from there I promoted myself into the business of manufacturing hair goods and preparations...I have built my own factory on my own ground."[4]

Right now, the most important thing for you to do is to take responsibility for your own actions or inactions, like Madame C. J. Walker and many others who persisted against the odds. Let go of the pride that says because of some reason-- (you fill in the blank), the world owes you something. You must accept the reality that there are forces in life that you will continue to encounter that will attempt to stifle your economic harvest. So substitute your pride, your security blanket like Charlie Brown did and get tired doing something productive, and I *guarantee* you will reap a harvest!

---

[4] Madame CJ Walker- The Official Website. December 1, 2010. http://www.madamcjwalker.com/

Reflection

Note to reader:

This is your opportunity to bring about a transformation in your life. I want to serve as your coach to assist you in walking through your trying times. If you want to change the direction your life is going, you must confront not only the enemies without, but more importantly the enemies the inner me(s) within. Following each step you will find a series of questions and/or fill in the blanks. The more honest you are with yourself, the sooner you can bring about a positive change in your life.

I want you to use these reflection segments at the end of each step as your personal journal to document your path of recovery. No one needs to see it but you. This is your opportunity to write your goals and desires on paper. Once you put them in writing you have taken the first step in breathing life into them. As you follow these steps faithfully, I stand in agreement with you that you can overcome your darkest fears and become the winner at life you were designed to be.

1. Who told you that you are not worthy of living a fulfilled and blessed life?

2. What have you identified as your blanket, your sense of security, and who stole if from you?

3. Have you let go of pride? Is pride keeping you from becoming all you can be?

4. What is your kryptonite that keeps you in bondage? What or who is it that you can't say "no" to even though you know it is destroying you?

5. Who hurt you physically, emotionally, psychologically, or spiritually?

6. Have you identified the enablers, the useless Snoopy dogs that you need to rid from your life?

7. If this was your last day on Earth, what are some of the things you would do? Now make a commitment to do one positive thing today towards achieving it, even if it is only in your imagination. Visualize yourself doing it now and believe that it can be yours as long as you never give up. (Make sure that this desire does not infringe upon the rights of others and that it is a legal and worthy attainment.)

Inspirational Nuggets

One of the first steps to take towards feeling whole is to know that you are loved, loveable, and that all your mistakes of the past are forgiven. These scriptures below continue to help me on my journey towards wholeness, self-acceptance, and forgiveness.

> Can a mother forget the baby at her breast and have no compassion on the child she has borne?
> Though she may forget,
> *I will not forget you*!
> See, I have engraved you on the palms of my hands; your walls are ever before me. Isaiah 49:15-16 (NIV)

> Beloved, I wish above all things *that thou mayest prosper and be in health, even as thy soul prospers* 3 John 1:2-3 (KJV)

> The thief comes only in order to steal and kill and destroy. I came that they may have and enjoy life, and have it in abundance (to the full, till it overflows). John 10:10 (AMP)

Notes

Step 2:

Stop Crying, "Woe is me!"

Like Linus

Gird up your loins now like a man; I will demand of you...

Job 40:7

Rise up, ye women that are at ease; ... Blessed are ye that sow beside all waters...

Isaiah 32: 9, 20

Life demands that sooner or later we must take a stand. Crying, "Woe is me (http://youtu.be/E7ID_E-SYbQ)!" continuously through life is a sure sign of immaturity.[5] It rains on the just and on the unjust. It doesn't matter whether you were born with a silver spoon in your mouth or no spoon at all. Clearly, it is not healthy to go through life constantly looking out your rear view mirror while trying to move forward.

We can all have a pity party and bring up the dramas and traumas that we have experienced. The question is-- what are you going to do about it now? We must decide whether we will become a victim of or a champion over our past.

---

[5] TickleMeCthulhu, *linus in withdrawals*. YouTube. December 1, 2010.

If we choose to become a victim, we will always have an excuse for our failures. As life proceeds, we can even attach layers like an onion to this core experience and blame this initial event for all of our subsequent ordeals or inability to achieve whatever goals we have set. It becomes a convenient excuse that no one will doubt its veracity. You now have a legitimate excuse and you can even label your experience as a byproduct of a "dysfunctional family or environment".

Society may embrace you and offer condolences, sympathy, empathy, or maybe a talk show appearance. However, there are very few individuals, who will tell you truthfully that you did suffer a calamity, but you must stop crying, "Woe is me!" Trustworthy friends will allow you to vent, encourage you to forgive your abusers, (and yourself if necessary), and will hold your hand if needed to help you move on with your life.

Beware however, of the dangers involved in becoming a champion over your past. Not everyone has a vested interest in seeing you leave your dysfunctional lifestyle behind. There are individuals, enablers, whose financial interest is tied up in victims maintaining their addiction, low self-esteem, depression, impoverished thoughts, etc. Please note that their career is based on you remaining in bondage.

Step One to regaining your lost income is to stop crying, "Woe is me!" Employers want to hire strong candidates who don't bring their emotional baggage to work. Get all the therapy and help that you need to keep yourself motivated and in a positive state of mind (I did). Join a support group if necessary.

Meditate and pray on your own. Ask God for the strength to forgive your enemies and move on with life.

Step Two involves assessing your strengths and weaknesses and applying for all jobs that interest you. In your spare time pursue your creative ideas. One of the tenets of life that I live by is the belief that built into each individual is the seed or potential to reproduce. I look at nature and it teaches me this truth; in every plant there is the capacity to survive, grow, and reproduce. What is fascinating about nature is that there are many ways that plants can produce new plants. Some of the ways that plants reproduce are by making their own seeds, or by creating new life without seeds by cuttings or graftings.

If nature, divine intelligence, or God, (I choose to accept the latter) has built into lower life the capacity to reproduce by various means, surely humans as the highest form of creation must likewise have the ability to survive, grow, reproduce, and thrive. Logic tells me that we have a brain in our cranium to think and to be creative for a purpose. We must use what is in us-- the seeds of intelligence, creativity, imagination, logic, emotion, forgiveness, wisdom, humor, communication, etc.-- *to not only survive, but to reproduce, and thrive.*

The problem for many of us is that we often don't use these seeds, these gifts, within us to prosper. Instead of seeing a crisis as a challenge, we see it as a setback. Instead of seeing poverty as a blessing-- an opportunity to become a millionaire like Chris

Gardner, author of *The Pursuit of Happyness*[6]-- we see it as a curse. Instead of seeing dermatitis as an opportunity to invent rubber gloves-- as Dr. William Stewart Halsted did-- we see it as an affliction. Yes, we truly have everything within us to prosper. It's a matter of how we see our situation-- is the cup half empty or half full? I choose to see the cup as half full and trust that God can and will make up the difference in my limitations. I believe that all of our cups are half full and that they are waiting to overflow, but we must initiate the process.

I hope that you are now fired up, and can see that the glass is really half full for you, and it is waiting to overflow. If so, I want you to pretend that you are independently wealthy. Turn now to the *Goal Setting Exercise* at the end of this chapter and write down on paper what you would do with your time. Describe what your goals are in life without questioning whether you can bring them to fruition or not. Don't procrastinate, and say I'll do it later. As Nike says, "just do it!"

Pioneering research on goal setting and motivation in the late 1960s by Dr. Edwin Locke entitled, "Toward a Theory of Task Motivation and Incentives,"[7] found that by setting SMART goals-- that are Specific, Measurable, Attainable, Relevant,

---

6 Gardner, Chris. (2006).*The Pursuit Of Happyness,* New York: Amistad. ISBN 978-0061138102

7 *Locke's Goal Setting Theory,* Mind Tools Ltd. December 1, 2010. - http://www.mindtools.com/pages/article/newHTE_87.htm

and Time-bound-- we will be well on our way to accomplishing them.[8]

Locke found that goal setting is a "powerful way of motivating people, and of motivating yourself. The value of goal setting is so well recognized that entire management systems, like 'Management by Objectives'[9], have goal setting basics incorporated within them. In fact, goal setting theory is generally accepted as among the most valid and useful motivation theories in industrial and organizational psychology, human resource management, and organizational behavior."[10]

Acknowledging this research, I'm sure you would agree that if you want to get across the Red Seas in your life, you must begin to work on your SMART goals today. Now look back at the *Goal Setting Exercise* at the end of this chapter and begin to do something today that is a step towards accomplishing one of your goals. Even if it is only a small baby step-- make the phone call, sign up for the course, or try out for the audition. What do you have to lose? At least when you reflect back later in life from your rocking chair, you can say I tried, and I did it my way. Your inability to fulfill your dream will not be from a lack of effort.

If your dream is to sing for the Pope and you do have some talent like Susan Boyle, then do it, even if you are homely looking and have only church choirs that embrace or tolerate you. Who knows? You may even get discovered like Susan or Fantasia

---

[8] Ibid., /page6.html.

[9] Ibid., /pages/article/newTMM_94.htm.

[10] Op.cit

Barrino and become a British or an American Idol or a world acclaimed star in your own right.

If your gifts are more cerebral or playful in nature, you may be fortunate enough to come up with the next rubber gloves, *Monopoly Game, Beanie Babies* or *Silly Bandz* toy invention! The key message in this step is to never give up! Nothing beats a failure but a try.

If you still need encouragement, peruse this selected list of individuals who became successful by failing over, and over, and over again:

- Thomas Edison's teachers said he was "too stupid to learn anything." He was fired from his first two jobs for being "non-productive." As an inventor, Edison made 1,000 unsuccessful attempts at inventing the light bulb. When a reporter asked, "How did it feel to fail 1,000 times?" Edison replied, "I didn't fail 1,000 times. The light bulb was an invention with 1,000 steps." (*He has been described as the greatest inventor who ever lived).*
- Henry Ford failed and went broke five times before he succeeded.
- Sigmund Freud was booed from the podium when he first presented his ideas to the scientific community of Europe. He returned to his office and kept on writing.
- R. H. Macy failed seven times before his store in New York City caught on.
- Michael Jordan and Bob Cousy were each cut from their high school basketball teams. Jordan once observed, 'I've failed over and over again in my life. That is why I succeed.'

- Babe Ruth is famous for his past home run record, but for decades he also held the record for strikeouts. He hit 714 home runs and struck out 1,330 times in his career (about which he said, 'Every strike brings me closer to the next home run.')
- Charles Schultz had every cartoon he submitted rejected by his high school yearbook staff. Oh, and Walt Disney wouldn't hire him.
- After his first audition, Sidney Poitier was told by the casting director, 'Why don't you stop wasting people's time and go out and become a dishwasher or something?' It was at that moment, recalls Poitier, that he decided to devote his life to acting.
- Beethoven handled the violin awkwardly and preferred playing his own compositions instead of improving his technique. His teacher called him 'hopeless as a composer.' And, of course, you know that he wrote five of his greatest symphonies while completely deaf.
- Louisa May Alcott, author of *Little Women*, was encouraged to find work as a servant by her family.
- Jack London (considered by many to be America's finest author) received six hundred rejection slips before he sold his first story.[11]

The obvious question is, "What have you failed at lately?" Have you been fired, left by a spouse, lost value in your stocks or pension, or been confined in

---

[11] *But They Did Not Give Up*, Emory University. December 1, 2010. http://www.des.emory.edu/mfp/efficacynotgiveup.html

an emotional and/or physical prison? If you can't come up with an answer than it stands to reason that perhaps you are not living up to your full potential. Perhaps you have not challenged yourself to explore the gifts, talents, desires, and dreams that are latent within you.

Ask yourself honestly whether you have reproduced something of value from within your loins. Have you "girded up your loins like a man [or woman]" and answered to the demands of the seed that is in you? The dictionary defines the word "loins" as follows: "to prepare oneself for something requiring readiness, strength, or endurance." The example it gives is: *He girded his loins to face his competitor.*

Have you risen up and sowed beside all waters? That is, dangerous, challenging waters that force you to launch out in the deep and walk on water as Peter did. Until you do, you will never discover Jesus' capacity to rescue you when the winds blow and you *perceive* that you are sinking.

Parenthetically, a recent example of the power of perseverance and faith was demonstrated during the recent internment of, the "los 33" Chilean miners who were sealed 2,300 feet underground by 700,000 tons of rock in a mine. They were quoted as saying that they were not "los 33", but "los 34" trapped in the mine. The 34th miner they said was God.

If your answer is "no", now is the time to get on board and prepare yourself for greatness.
Like Edison, Ford, Thomas, Ruth, London, the Chilean miners, and many others. You too can gird your loins, sow beside all waters, face your competitors, leave a legacy, and reproduce

something of greatness for the world to see, enjoy, or benefit from. Like the "los 33", you too can call on God when your hope is bleak, your strength is gone, and all you can say or think of is, "Woe is me!"

Reflection

1. How often do you cry, "Woe is me?" Are you ready to stop crying, "Woe is me!"?

2. Have you chosen to be a victim or a champion over your past? Describe how you will take control of the dark forces in your life.

3. Do you want to get well? Do you believe that you can be made whole in mind, body, soul, and spirit? What makes you say this? Support your beliefs in writing below.

4. Have you taken responsibility for your stolen blanket? How long are you going to sit crying out like the man at the pool of Bethesda (John 5:1-18) waiting for someone to give you that push so that you can be healed?

5. Have you had a face to face encounter in the mirror with yourself? What was the revelation?

6. Do you need help, and if so, have you sincerely asked for it? (Please note that there are agencies and resources in the appendix of this book that will help you to get back on the success track.)

7. Is your cup half empty or half full? What are you doing *today* about it?

8. Goal Setting Exercise: Pretend right now that you are independently wealthy. Write in the space below what you would do with your time. Describe what your goals are in life right now without questioning whether you can bring them to fruition or not. Don't procrastinate, and say I'll do it later. Write down your thoughts now.

Inspirational Nuggets

The following scriptures helped me to stop crying, "Woe is me." They inspired me to try again, to believe with God's help I could achieve greater successes. They challenged me to believe that my past failures, disadvantages, ostracisms, or negative experiences were not an indication of my destiny in life. Instead I saw them as a sign that I had survived and the foundation had been set deep--like one that is made for a tall building--so that I could stand erect and soar to great heights. These obstacles of the past have been a blessing in disguise. My overcoming them has allowed me to triumph and help others realize the greatness that is within them.

These verses gave me the assurance that God's will for me was an abundant life that included prosperity, wisdom, health, a sound mind, and all my financial needs being met. They inspired me to believe that I could begin again. They gave me a sense of hope and a belief that I had a positive future ahead of me.

> "Behold, I make all things new." Revelation 21:5

> "With men this is impossible; but with God all things are possible." Matthew 19:26

Ask, and it shall be given you; seek, and ye shall find; knock, and it shall be opened unto you: Matthew 7:7

Notes

Step 3

Don't Look for Snoopy

to Rescue You!

"Prince Charming only exists in fairy tales."

Anonymous

Most children, particularly girls, in the Western world do not escape childhood without hearing the story of Cinderella (http://youtu.be/dd0fuaD-OwE) read to them.[12] It's a classic rags-to-riches story about a knight in shining armor who rescues a servant girl named Cinderella, who is mistreated by her mean step-mother and her two step-sisters. Thousands of variants of this classic folk tale are known however throughout the world. They portray how a young woman suffering unjust oppression is suddenly rewarded and receives a remarkable fortune.[13]

The *Cinderella Complex* was first described by Colette Dowling, who wrote a book on women's fear of independence, as an unconscious desire to be taken care of by others, based primarily on a fear of

---

[12] Rajshri, *Fairy Tales- Cinderella.* YouTube. December 1, 2010.

[13] ^ Zipes, Jack (2001). *The Great Fairy Tale Tradition: From Straparola and Basile to the Brothers Grimm.* W. W. Norton & Co. p. 444. ISBN 978-0393976366

being independent.[14] The complex is said to become more apparent as a person grows older.

This complex is named after the fairy tale character Cinderella, popularized by the Disney movie of the same name.[15] It is based on the portrayal of women as being only beautiful, graceful, and polite. However, they cannot be strong independent characters themselves unless like Cinderella, they are in hot pursuit of a man. Cinderella is virtually seen as a weak, defenseless female that is nothing without a man.

Although the story of Cinderella is a fairy tale, it dangerously mirrors the stereotypical choices many females make as they approach and transition from adolescence to adulthood. The following statistics on romance fiction corroborates the extent to which females continue to be influenced by fairy tales even as adults. 2010 Romance Writers of America, Inc. reported the following statistics on their website:

> ... romance fiction generated $1.37 billion in sales in 2008, but also it remained the *largest share of the consumer market* at 13.5 percent. R.R. Bowker's Books In Print shows 7,311 new romance titles were published in the United States in 2008 (out of a total 275,232 new titles). With 7,311 new romances

---

[14] Colette Dowling (1990). *The Cinderella Complex: Women's Hidden Fear of Independence.* Simon & Schuster. ISBN 0671733346

[15] *Cinderella (1950 film)*, Wikipedia The Free Encyclopedia. December 1, 2010. - http://en.wikipedia.org/wiki/Cinderella_(1950_film)

published in one year, 'no fiction category can rival romance in terms of sheer size.'[16]

The article goes on to point out that these, "romance novels are titles that are aimed mostly at women, who read 90.5 percent of all romance novels. Their offering at a low price point helped make romance the number one category on best-seller lists in 2008."[17] Is it any wonder that girls and women are described as being more co-dependent than males?

Although there are males that are co-dependent, most people would agree that this is not a syndrome that would be used to describe males. Most men do not look for a knight (or princess) in shining armor to rescue them. Society, literature, and Judeo-Christian theology generally teach and reinforce that, "If a man will not work, he shall not eat." (2 Thessalonians 3:10 NIV).

Because of the gravity of this phenomenon in regards to women, my focus in this section is primarily aimed at helping females to reframe their thinking in terms of how to handle a job crisis, lay off, loss of income from a spouse or partner, or a lack of education, training, and experience. The information of course, is equally beneficial for males.

---

[16] Norris, Michael, Warren Pawlowski, eds. *Business of Consumer Book Publishing 2009.* (Stamford: Simba Information, 2009), 175

[17] *2009 RWA Reader Survey*, Romance Writers of America. December 1, 2010, http://www.rwanational.org/cs/readership_stats.

Many songs in our culture reinforce this syndrome as well. So much so, that this myth of the helpless female is passed along innocuously from generation to generation through music. Take a look at this classic song that Dean Martin made famous:

> You're nobody 'til somebody loves you
> You're nobody 'til somebody cares.
> You may be king, you may possess the world and its gold,
> But gold won't bring you happiness when you're growing old.
> The world still is the same, you never change it,
> As sure as the stars shine above;
> ***You're nobody 'til somebody loves you***,
> So find yourself somebody to love.
>
> The world still is the same, you never change it,
> As sure as the stars shine above;
> You're nobody 'til somebody loves you,
> So find yourself somebody, find yourself somebody,
> ***Find yourself somebody to love.***[18]

Incidentally, I can recall in college that a classmate of mine told me that she attended college so that she could get a "Mrs." behind her name as opposed to a "Masters degree". Her goal was realized and one month before graduation she married a man that she later divorced after a short marital sprint.

---

[18] *Dean Martin- You're Nobody Till Somebody Loves You Lyrics.* STLyrics. December 1, 2010. http://www.stlyrics.com/lyrics/swingers/yourenobodytillsomebodylovesyou.htm

How about this modern day version of Dean Martin's song entitled, *Single Ladies* by Beyonce? It's a song written specifically for single women who desire-- you guessed it-- a man above all things in life. Take a good look at the lyrics, without the beat and Beyonce's voluptuous body gyrating all over the stage:

All the single ladies, all the single ladies
All the single ladies, all the single ladies
All the single ladies, all the single ladies
All the single ladies

Now put your hands up
Up in the club, we just broke up
I'm doing my own little thing...

Just cried my tears, for three good years...
Cause if you liked it then you should have put a ring on it...
I got gloss on my lips, a man on my hips
Got me tighter in my Dereon jeans...

I need no permission, did I mention
Don't pay him any attention
Cause you had your turn and now you gonna learn...

Don't treat me to the things of the world
I'm not that kind of girl
Your love is what I prefer, what I deserve

Here's a *man that makes me* then takes me
And *delivers me to a destiny, to infinity and beyond*
Pull me into your arms, *say I'm the one you own*

If you don't, you'll be alone....[19]

"*Delivers me to a destiny, to infinity and beyond*"? What are we teaching our daughters about life, reality, or responsibility? Is there any promotion of women taking care of themselves, pursuing education, buying a home, starting a business, investing in stocks, bonds, or themselves, etc.? Whatever happened to loving yourself...? You may have the greatest, most sensitive, caring husband in the world, but what happens when he dies ladies?

Most women do outlive men, so how can you be somebody, when your lover dies, or leaves, becomes ill, or finds a younger version of you? Have you developed the skills to support yourself, and your children if necessary? Love does make the world go round, sells tons of CDs and spandex, but money, a secure income, and most importantly a healthy sense of self, help a whole lot!

My advice is to-- ***stop looking for Prince Charming to rescue you, he doesn't exist!*** Look instead at what the research and statistics reveal to us in an article written by Terry Savage, a Sun-Times Columnist, entitled, "Harsh Statistics Should Propel Women To Plan Ahead."[20] Her report should be viewed as a wake-up call for women who are still looking for Prince Charming to rescue them.

---

[19] *Single Ladies lyrics*. Elyrics. December 1, 2010. http://www.elyrics.net/read/b/beyonce-lyrics/single-ladies-lyrics.html

[20] Chicago Sun-Times. December 1, 2010. http://www.suntimes.com/business/savage/2292120-452/women-financial-percent-retirement-filings.html

Some key points that Ms. Savage made were that, "women live longer, earn less, have fewer retirement assets, and suffer longer periods of debilitating illness in their old age. Many financial problems faced by women are created by divorce. Women make up 75 percent of the elderly poor today. Perhaps that's because one of every two women over 65 is divorced or widowed."

Another shocking statistic mentioned in this same article came found from the General Accounting Office. It states that, "80 percent of women living in poverty were not poor before their husbands died. These women come from a generation that was not encouraged to learn about financial issues, and they had little opportunity to create economic independence."

These statistics should make it clear to the reader that education, redirection, and a refocus on women's empowerment are vitally needed. Since the penning of her article dated, August 7, 2001, the economic plight for women has only gotten worse due to the recession which according to the *National Bureau of Economic Research* (the official arbiter of recessions) began in December 2007.[21]

It is said that history repeats itself, and if we don't learn the lesson, we will continue to make the same mistake generation, after generation. The iconic Billie Holliday tried to warn women of this truth towards the end of the Great Depression in her rendering of the classic song, *God Bless the Child*:

---

21 *It's official: Recession since Dec. '07.* CNN Money. December 1. 2010.

Them that's got shall get
Them that's not shall lose
So the Bible said and it still is news
Mama may have, Papa may have
But God bless the child that's got his own
That's got his own

Yes, the strong gets more
While the weak ones fade
Empty pockets don't ever make the grade
Mama may have, Papa may have
But God bless the child that's got his own
That's got his own

Money, you've got lots of friends
Crowding round the door
When you're gone, spending ends
They don't come no more
Rich relations give
Crust of bread and such
You can help yourself
But don't take too much
Mama may have, Papa may have
But God bless the child that's got his own
That's got his own....[22]

The song, "*God Bless the Child*", written by Billie Holiday[23] and Arthur Herzog, Jr. in 1939 has stood the test of time for its enduring message that is just as relevant today, if not more, than it was during the early 1930s. It was honored with the Grammy

---

[22] *God Bless The Child lyrics*. Elyrics. December 1, 2010. http://www.elyrics.net/read/b/billie-holiday-lyrics/god-bless-the-child-lyrics.html

[23] *Billie Holiday*. Wikipedia The Free Encyclopedia. December 1, 2010. http://en.wikipedia.org/wiki/Billie_Holiday

Hall of Fame Award (1976) and was also included in the list of Songs of the Century[24], by the Recording Industry Association of America and the National Endowment for the Arts.

My strong recommendations to women who are attempting to rebuild their life after an income loss are as follows:

- ✓ Pursue your dreams!
- ✓ Go as far as you can in the completion of a formal education.
- ✓ Become a lifelong learner.
- ✓ Invest your money, time, and talent in fruitful ventures.
- ✓ Constantly acquire skills that will allow you to *compete globally in any economic market.*
- ✓ Get a good husband if that is your desire (I have one, I love him dearly and wouldn't trade him). Two incomes are always better than one! I'm sure any single woman can attest to this, especially since there is still disparity between what women and men are paid.
- ✓ Make sure that what you have is *your own.* Acquire the copyright, trademark, patent, deed, and make sure that in your will the word, "perpetuity", is included, which means for eternity or the rest of time. In this way you have a legacy that you can control from the grave.

Please note that these suggestions are not necessarily in chronological order, but should be acquired during a woman's lifetime.

---

[24] Ibid., /Strange_Fruit

Reflection

1. Are you still waiting for Prince Charming to sweep you off your feet and make your life better? Is this person real or a figment of your imagination?

2. Do you have a co-dependent personality? If so, how does it manifest itself? List the individuals that you think you can't live without or that can't live without you.

3. Would you choose nine times out of ten to read a romance novel rather than a book on financial planning? Why?

4. Have you accepted responsibility for yourself and stopped blaming others? How did you come to this realization?

5. Have you worked out a budget detailing your income, assets and expenses? Write down what it is.

6. If your spouses' income stopped, would you be able to support yourself and the family? Write down how you would do it.

7. Who is in your corner partnering with you? Is your relationship mutually beneficial or is it a co-dependent one?

8. List below what you possess that you can call "your own".

9. What job or entrepreneurial skills do you possess that will allow you to compete in a global marketplace today? List them now, as well as your gifts, talents, hobbies, and the things you do naturally that others applaud you for or will pay to have you perform these talents.

Inspirational Nuggets

I began to mature and see progress in my life when I gave up my rescue fantasies, magical thinking, and beliefs that just being lucky or sexy would cause what I wanted to materialize into my existence. I used visualization along with determined, purposeful behavior to bring about the successes in my life. Like Ruth of the Bible, who lost her husband-- her means of livelihood--I had to get out into the world and reap the sheaves being left behind.

Reaping involved studying, applying myself, partnering with others, working hard, and receiving the favor of God. The scriptures below instructed and inspired me to change, to use the gifts and talents I possessed to expand them into something greater, more profitable.

> You will pray to him, and he will hear you,
> and you will fulfill your vows to him.
> You will succeed in whatever you choose to do, and light will shine on the road ahead of you.
> Job 22:27-29 (NLT)

> She goes to inspect a field and buys it;
> with her earnings she plants a vineyard.
> She is energetic and strong, a hard worker.
> She makes sure her dealings are profitable;
> her lamp burns late into the night.
> Proverbs 31:16-18 (NLT)

Notes

Step 4:

Stay Away From Lucy's 5¢ Psychiatric Help Booth

Then Job answered and said I have heard many such things: *miserable comforters* are ye all.

Job 16:1-2

"You get what you pay for!", so the saying goes. I don't know who the author is, but he or she was on target. When you have suffered an income loss-- the rent or mortgage is due, and the baby needs a new pair of shoes-- you must exercise extreme caution when accepting advice from others. Your goal is to gain long-term employment as quickly as possible from a reputable agency, firm, or a self-employment venture. I want to give you some do's and don'ts. I'll start first with the "Don'ts":

1. Don't listen to the counsel of someone you have to pay a specific, ironclad price to get advice. If you seek the advice of a financial counselor, a reputable one should see you on a sliding scale fee system if you are experiencing a severe economic hardship.

2. Anything involving luck or chance is not a solid solution to your financial situation. Stay away from Lucy's 5¢ Psychiatric Help Booth

(http://youtu.be/h38srxvt6qE)[25], the Lottery, Bingo, horse/dog races, individuals who read cards, tell your future or fortune by looking in crystal balls, or give advice on Psychic Hotlines, etc.

3. Don't respond to late night offers or once in a lifetime deals that expire at an exact time. Steer clear of offers that don't allow you to check with trusted friends, relatives, or someone who has your best interests in mind.

4. Don't sign contracts that you have to give substantial percentages of your future earnings for *perpetuity* (this word means forever!).

5. Don't sign contracts if you don't understand every single word in it or you have the slightest doubt about what you are doing or signing up for. Take it to a trusted friend, teacher, or attorney and find out what the words mean.

6. Don't move forward, if the individual or firm won't let you think about or pray about it overnight. If they are condescending or criticize you for wanting to think over or pray about it, definitely do not do business with these individuals.

7. Don't make a decision when you are depressed, tired or while you are under the influence of alcohol or drugs.

---

[25] TickleMeCthulhu, *Lucy Analyzes Charlie Brown.* YouTube. December 1, 2010.

8. Don't associate with people who are down on their luck and won't do anything to improve their situation. Remember the saying-- "misery likes miserable company."

9. Turn off the negative news, reports, or statistics that reinforce and reiterate that things are bad or predict that things will get worse. Remember that during the Great Depression everyone was not broke, and some creative individuals became millionaires!

10. Don't sell your gold *unless it is scrap* and there is no possible use for it! If your jewelry is a set or a decorative piece, a reputable jeweler would probably give you a whole lot more because they can resell it, versus a company that will melt it down into a bar. It's important to keep your family heirlooms! Remember your financial crisis is temporary—things will and have always gotten better.

Let's define now what good counsel looks like. These are the "*Do's*" that you should cling to:

1. Do seek the advice from trusted friends, family members, ministers, counselors, etc. that have a vested interest in your goodwill and not a vested financial interest.

2. When responding to offers for online schools and training programs, check to see if they

are accredited with officially recognized national agencies and institutions.

3. Check with the Better Business Bureau (and other industry specific accreditation or licensing agencies) for complaints, years in the business, customer ratings, resolutions of conflicts, etc.

4. Conduct an Internet Google search, such as "accreditation, financial, servicing, employment, etc. problems with ABC agency, school, or organization."

5. When in doubt, think about, pray or meditate on your decision before moving forward.

6. Stay current and read, read, read-- especially biographies about individuals and groups that have overcome adversities!

7. Associate with people who encourage and show appreciation for your natural gifts and talents. Find your passion and do what you love to do better than anyone else and you will find great reward! Remember, your financial crisis is temporary.

8. Pray and meditate daily. Ask God for witty inventions. Proverbs 8:12 states, "I wisdom dwell with prudence, and find out knowledge of witty inventions." Job 33:15-16, tells us that God speaks to us in dreams and visions and gives us assignments for the betterment of mankind as follows: "In a dream, in a vision of the night, when deep sleep falleth upon men, in slumberings upon the bed; then he

openeth the ears of men, and sealeth their instruction..."

9. If you are inspired by a dream, like Madame C. J. Walker or Bill Gates, keep it to yourself! Research the idea and find out all you can about it. Ask yourself-- is there a need for it? Pursue the idea in your spare time. Are you passionate about it? Some ideas or products take years to bring to fruition. Extensively research the process of obtaining an exclusive patent, trademark or copyright. Check with the U.S. Copyright Office[26] and United States Patent and Trademark Office[27] and then get it in your name so that you have ownership and control!

Did you know that Charles Darrow, a once unemployed salesman, who struggled with odd jobs to support his family, years following the great stock market crash of 1929 became a millionaire from the royalties he received as the founder of Hasbro's Monopoly game? There is still to this day much controversy however about whether he was the actual inventor.

Many accounts attribute Elizabeth Magie as the inventor for designing "The Landlord's Game", which is supposedly the ancestor of Monopoly. What Mr. Darrow did do-- and this is why he became a millionaire-- he made the game marketable, secured a copyright for this game in 1933, and acquired a patent in 1935. Parker Brothers subsequently acquired the patent and began to publish and sell

---

[26] http://www.copyright.gov/

[27] http://www.uspto.gov/

Monopoly. At some point in 1936, Parker Brothers was selling 20,000 copies of the game every week. Accordingly, this enabled Darrow to become the first millionaire game designer during the Great Depression.[28]

Was Elizabeth Magie's blanket stolen by Charles Darrow? Was she short-changed? Charles Darrow is the man given credit for the creation of Monopoly. He changed the rules and some of the layout from Lizzie Magie's version and got a patent put on it and then sold it to Parker Bros.

What we can learn from history, and history does repeat itself, is that you must learn the societal rules and its laws. It is especially important that once you obtain the copyright, trademark, and patent for your idea or invention, you obtain honest legal representation.

If you notice, I have advised that you obtain legal representation after you have done due diligence and obtained the copyright and patent *in your name first* before you secure legal representation or sell your patent. The danger in going to a manufacturer or attorney is that they can tweak your product or idea and make it theirs. Some say that this is what Mr. Darrow did to Elizabeth Magie's invention of The Landlord's Game. Who knows? It is clear however, that we can learn a lesson from this and make sure we protect our rights to our ideas, dreams, and inventions.

---

[28] Erik Arneson, *Charles Darrow- Board Game Designer Biography*. About.com. December 1, 2010. http://tinyurl.com/4m7eoab

To sum up, make sure you avoid the quacks that only want your money, are primarily concerned about themselves, or want pawns that they can control. Read all you can, never stop learning, exercise due diligence, and get the copyright, trademark, or patent in your exclusive name, for you and your heirs. Always seek the counsel of only qualified individuals who are trustworthy, professional or licensed, and have your best interests in mind! Pray always. Personally, I have found that my best counselor is Jesus. He has been the real friend who sticks closer than a brother (Proverbs 18:24 NLT).

Reflection

1. Do you believe in luck? If so, describe how it will make your dreams come true?

2. What thoughts are you meditating on regularly? List them and rate the quality of them. Are they helping you to advance in life?

3. Have you been hanging out at Lucy's 5¢ Psychiatric Help Booth? If so, detail what you have learned from going there.

4. Who is/are the Lucy(s) in your life that you need to walk away from?

5. What type of counseling advice have you been receiving? Detail the pros and cons of your adviser(s). Why do you trust them? How have they proven themselves to be reliable?

6. Are your advisers qualified, trustworthy, and licensed if necessary to give advice?

7. Have you eliminated the naysayers from your life? Individuals that think you will always be "broke, busted and disgusted". Who are they? Have you gotten rid of so-called friends that don't believe in your dreams?

8. Have you turned a deaf ear to family members that think that your genetic DNA is incapable of greatness, witty inventions, stable and fulfilling employment? If you still live with them, what are the ways that you cope? How can you overcome their negative forecasts?

9. In the presence of your enemies, detail how do you plan to advance your dreams. What are the positive forecasts that you tell yourself? Speak greatness to yourself now and tell the obstacles in your life that they will no longer torment you (Matthew 17:19-21 NIV).

Inspirational Nuggets

Sometimes, like Dorothy in the Wizard of Oz we get desperate and just want someone to show us how to get to our treasured destination. We want someone to pronounce on us that this is our vocation and we will have great success when we pursue this occupation.

I found however, through trial and error like Dorothy, that the wizard is really inside of us. Yes, we can and do acquire friendships, acquaintances, advisers, and counselors along the road of life that can help steer us in the right direction. But, the problem with relying on an individual is that they ultimately can't see the gifts that are locked up inside of us. They can give us a certain degree of direction, but like the caterpillar, we must personally go through the metamorphic changes in order to become a mature, majestic masterpiece that can fly by our own volition.

When we are able to do this, then we can assume ownership, and it's ours. No one can write our story, we have written it through our own experiences. It becomes our "auto" biography as opposed to a biography. We can now sing along with Billie Holliday because we have become the blessed child that has "their own".

The verses below inspired me to leave my comfort zone and develop my wings so that I could soar and become all that I desired to be based on my genetic and preordained potential.

All the advice you receive has made you tired.
Where are all your astrologers,
those stargazers who make predictions each month?
Let them stand up and save you from what the future holds.
But they are like straw burning in a fire;
they cannot save themselves from the flame.
You will get no help from them at all;
their hearth is no place to sit for warmth
(Isaiah 47:13-14 NLT).

Where no counsel is, the people fall: but in the multitude of counselors there is safety. Proverbs 11:14

Blessed is the man that walks not in the counsel of the ungodly...And he shall be like a tree planted by the rivers of water, that brings forth his fruit in his season; his leaf also shall not wither; and whatsoever he doeth shall prosper. Psalm 1:1-3

Notes

Step 5:

Keep Moving!

...Write the vision, and make *it* plain upon tables, *that he may run*....For the vision *is* yet for an appointed time...though it tarry, wait for it; because it will surely come, *it will not tarry.*

Habakkuk 2:2-3

For many Americans, not only is their money funny-- they have lost the security blanket of a "good job", or "good income from a spouse"-- but also that treasured hourglass or six-pack ab figure is now gone. What makes it worse is that this lost physique is now costing them more in terms of *money, job security, job advancement, relationships, and their general health.*

To prove my point, let's look first at the research on the medical effects and costs associated with obesity. Secondly, we will look at the research correlations between job security, career advancement, relationships, and obesity.

I Googled the words, "weight loss" and I came up with 485,000,000 results as of the writing of this book. During the past 20 years there has been a dramatic increase in obesity in the United States, so it's no wonder that these two words, "weight loss" would get over 485,000,000 hits.

The Journal of the American Medical Association concluded in an article entitled, *Prevalence and*

Trends in Obesity Among US Adults, 1999-2008[29], that "in 2007-2008, the prevalence of obesity was 32.2% among adult men and 35.5% among adult women. The increases in the prevalence of obesity previously observed do not appear to be continuing at the same rate over the past 10 years, particularly for women and possibly for men."

A study by the CDC entitled, "*Obesity by Race/Ethnicity 2006-2008*,"[30] found that although obesity may be slowing down in the U.S., new obesity data shows that African-Americans however, have the highest rates of obesity. This study found that:

> Blacks had 51 percent higher prevalence of obesity, and Hispanics had 21 percent higher obesity prevalence compared with whites.
>
> Greater prevalences of obesity for blacks and whites were found in the South and Midwest than in the West and Northeast. Hispanics in the Northeast had lower obesity prevalence than Hispanics in the Midwest, South or West.

Let's look first at the medical effects and financial costs of obesity, and then reflect on what the research shows us in terms of job security, work

---

[29] JAMA, Journal of the American Medical Association. December 1, 2010. http://jama.ama-assn.org/content/303/3/235.short

[30] Center for Disease Control and Prevention. December 1, 2010. http://www.cdc.gov/obesity/data/trends.html#Race

bias, career advancement, and overall interpersonal relationships. Stanford Hospitals and Clinic reported the following findings in an article entitled, *Health Effects of Obesity*:[31]

> Obesity has a far-ranging negative effect on health. Each year obesity-related conditions cost over 150 billion dollars and cause an estimated 300,000 premature deaths in the US. The health effects associated with obesity include, but are not limited to, the following:
>
> **high blood pressure** - Additional fat tissue in the body needs oxygen and nutrients in order to live, which requires the blood vessels to circulate more blood to the fat tissue. This increases the workload of the heart because it must pump more blood through additional blood vessels. More circulating blood also means more pressure on the artery walls. Higher pressure on the artery walls increases the blood pressure. In addition, extra weight can raise the heart rate and reduce the body's ability to transport blood through the vessels.
>
> **diabetes** - Obesity is the major cause of type 2 diabetes. This type of diabetes usually begins in adulthood but, is now actually occurring in children....
>
> **heart disease** - Atherosclerosis (hardening of the arteries) is present 10 times more often in

[31] Stanford Hospital & Clinics. December 1, 2010. http://stanfordhospital.org/clinicsmedServices/COE/surgicalServices/generalSurgery/bariatricsurgery/obesity/effects.html

obese people compared to those who are not obese. Coronary artery disease is also more prevalent because fatty deposits build up in arteries that supply the heart. Narrowed arteries and reduced blood flow to the heart can cause chest pain (angina) or a heart attack. Blood clots can also form in narrowed arteries and cause a stroke.

joint problems, including osteoarthritis - Obesity can affect the knees and hips because of the stress placed on the joints by extra weight....

sleep apnea and respiratory problems - Sleep apnea, which causes people to stop breathing for brief periods, interrupts sleep throughout the night and causes sleepiness during the day. It also causes heavy snoring....

cancer - In women, being overweight contributes to an increased risk for a variety of cancers including breast, colon, gallbladder, and uterus. Men who are overweight have a higher risk of colon and prostate cancers.

metabolic syndrome - The National Cholesterol Education Program has identified metabolic syndrome as a complex risk factor for cardiovascular disease. Metabolic syndrome consists of six major components: abdominal obesity, elevated blood cholesterol, elevated blood pressure, insulin resistance with or without glucose intolerance, elevation of certain blood components that indicate

> inflammation, and elevation of certain clotting factors in the blood. In the US, approximately one-third of overweight or obese persons exhibit metabolic syndrome.

The medical costs of obesity are staggering as well. Steven Reinberg, HealthDay Reporter for ABC NEWS, revealed in an article entitled, *Almost 10 Percent of U.S. Medical Costs Tied to Obesity,* [32] that:

> Obesity in the United States now carries the hefty price tag of $147 billion per year in direct medical costs, just over 9 percent of all medical spending, experts report.
>
> In fact, people who are obese spend almost $1,500 more each year on health care -- about 41 percent more than an average-weight person. Beyond those costs are the disability and early deaths caused by obesity, Dr. Thomas R. Frieden, director of the U.S. Centers for Disease Control and Prevention said...
>
> 'Obesity, and with it diabetes, are the only major health problems that are getting worse in this country, and they are getting worse rapidly,' Frieden said. 'The average American is now 23 pounds overweight.'

Reinberg goes on in this article to point out that the remedy for this obesity epidemic and escalating

[32] abc NEWS. December 1, 2010 (http://tinyurl.com/nujn6x).

medical costs according to experts is a return to healthy behaviors.

A corroborating study entitled, *Body Weight – A 'Heavy' Influence on Career Success,*[33] conducted at Wayne State University in Detroit, MI, showed that, yes, obesity can and does have a denigrating effect in the workplace. Part of the report's findings was the following:

> 'There are a whole set of stereotypes that go along with being overweight, and a lot of them transfer into the workplace in terms of people's judgment about others' abilities and appearance in relation to job performance,' said doctoral candidate Cort Rudolph.
>
> Researchers have studied the effects of weight–based bias in the workplace for more than 30 years, and Rudolph has completed a meta–analysis of many of the findings. 'The results have been consistent. People who are overweight are viewed more negatively in the workplace than those who are of average weight, which is not surprising based on what we know about weight-based stereotypes,' he said.
>
> Some of the basic stereotypes associated with being overweight include laziness, sloppiness, untidiness and lack of self–discipline and control. Overweight people are also regularly labeled as having increased health problems,

[33] Society For Industrial & Organizational Psychology, Inc. December 1, 2010." (http://tinyurl.com/4dln3ee)

> which is an issue often considered cumbersome by organizations....
>
> But there is some good news for overweight employees. The bias effect tends to decrease as people's tenure with an organization increases, Rudolph said.
>
> In his study he found that stereotypes are most prominent in the initial selection process. Body weight seems to be less of a factor at the performance evaluation stage, and stereotypes have a minimum influence when it comes to promotions.

Obesity also affects our interpersonal relationships and transfers to the workplace as well, sometimes resulting in job discrimination. In the article previously cited entitled, "Health Effects of Obesity,"[34] researchers found the following to be true concerning the psychosocial effects of obesity:

> In a culture where often the ideal of physical attractiveness is to be overly thin, people who are overweight or obese frequently suffer disadvantages. Overweight and obese persons are often blamed for their condition and may be considered to be lazy or weak-willed. It is not uncommon for overweight or obese conditions to result in persons having lower incomes or having fewer or no romantic relationships. Disapproval of overweight persons expressed by some individuals may

---

[34] Ibid.

progress to bias, discrimination, and even torment.

To the reader it should be crystal clear at this point that there is a tremendous cost associated with not moving and having a sedentary lifestyle. Our bodies are designed to move, work, exercise, and take in foods that foster health and nutrition. The absence of such not only affects our income, but our health, ability to secure a job, as well as social and romantic relationships. The above research plainly conveys that commitment to a healthy lifestyle and exercise program is vitally important.

I have a motto I live by that helps me get through the *mean times* in my life. This is what I recommend that you do-- in your "*meantime(s)*"-- while you are waiting for the job offer, the academic or medical test results, or an acceptance letter for admittance into an institution of higher learning, etc. I want to pass on its beneficial effects to you the reader. It is two simple words, "**KEEP MOVING**!" It's an acrostic that stands for:

Keep current with today's issues and trends. Become a lifelong learner.
Exercise daily and eat healthy foods.
Encourage yourself, even if no one else does.
Pray often for God's strength and that his plan to prosper you and keep you in good health will be manifested in your life. Follow God's Word.

Music and laughter are said to be the elixir of life. Proverbs 17:22 states that "A merry heart doeth good like a medicine..." According to an article entitled, *How Music Affects Us and*

Promotes Health,[35] there are many benefits associated with listening to music. A few of its many attributes include: the ability to facilitate healing, reduce pain, release endorphins, reduce blood pressure, boost your immune system, decrease levels of stress-related hormone cortisol, enhance intelligence, improve concentration and memory, and improve athletic performance. The importance of making music and laughter a part of your everyday life cannot be over emphasized.

Open yourself to experiences that challenge you to grow, think, imagine, and use your creativity.

Visualize your dreams coming true, don't look back, and don't take "no," for an answer. Believe that with God's help all things are possible! Practice the *Serenity Prayer*, and learn when to persevere and when to let go.

Invest your money and time in ventures that will allow you to leave a positive legacy. Pay your bills on time and use credit sparingly and wisely. Before making a major investment, investigate thoroughly before turning over your earnings to someone else!

Never give up! As long as you keep trying, there is always hope.

Give to others who are in need and inspire them with your stories of victory. Always be quick to forgive yourself, others, and allow them the benefit of the doubt.

In order to run with your vision, dreams, goals, hopes, and desires, it is essential that you maintain a healthy lifestyle. This is particularly important as

---

[35] eMedExpert. December 1, 2010. (http://tinyurl.com/dyqteg)

you approach mid-life and your senior years. The retirement age is being gradually pushed back into the late 60s and for some individuals, the 70s. Employers want individuals who are physically, mentally, and morally strong that can keep the company's bottom line in the black. Even if you are doing well as a self-employed business owner or if you are financially independent, what good is your money if you can't enjoy it because of illness?

In a nutshell, always remember that when sickness, poverty, depression, unemployment, under-employment, a natural disaster, or discouragement attempt to bring you down, if you keep moving in the "***mean times***", these calamities can't attack your body, mind, soul, or spirit as long as you ***KEEP MOVING!***

Reflection

1. Do you have any diet, weight or health challenges that interfere with your ability to advance in life, find a job and keep it? If so, write down your plan to eliminate them?

2. How often do you work out weekly? Are you pleased with this amount of time you devote to taking care of yourself? If not, commit now in writing how you will change your schedule?

3. What do you do daily to prevent obesity in your family tree? If you have children, are you making sure they are not acquiring habits that will cause them to be overweight?

4. Do you see a doctor regularly? Have you been advised to change your diet or lifestyle? If yes, write down a plan you should be following daily.

5. Have your social relationships suffered as a result of any health or weight problems? How can you change this situation today?

6. Do you find yourself alone frequently watching television and eating junk food? Are they your best friends? If so, what is your plan to find friends who are fun to be around and make good health choices?

7. How often do you listen to relaxing music or meditate? Do you need to increase your intake of both of these?

8. Is there anyone you need to forgive? Are you holding on to bitter past experiences that still have you in bondage? Write down now what or who you need to release from your life. Do you need to forgive yourself?

9. For some individuals after several weeks, months, or years without a positive job offer, signs of frustration begin to build up. Negative telltale signs can manifest during subsequent interviews as depression, aggression, nervousness, or unconsciously rejecting yourself before the interviewer can reject you. Do you reject yourself or set yourself up for rejection? Write down how you should prepare yourself for interviews.

10. Is the pursuit of money your main objective in life? If so, how can you remedy this so that you have a balanced, peaceful life?

11. Do you have any abusive behavior or addictions (to food, money, gambling, sex, drugs, alcohol, prescription medications, etc.) that keep you in bondage and prevent you from advancing in your career or in life?

Inspirational Nuggets

Below are two different scenarios of groups of people who were impotent in body and in finances. The first group was waiting by the pool for someone to move the waters (the calamities, the challenges, the illnesses) so that their security blanket could be restored and they could be made whole again. The second group facing famine and certain death took a different approach. They mustered the courage to keep moving in order to make their situation better. They reasoned that it was better to keep trying, rather than give up and face death without a valiant attempt to defeat their enemies.

The first group below was waiting for someone to move things for them. In contrast, the second group realized that they had been given authority and dominion to move and defeat all living things. As co-creators with God they exercised their right to change dark situations into positive ones. They had faith and refused to give up without a courageous attempt to rectify their situation.

> In these (the pool of Bethesda) lay a great multitude of impotent folk, of blind, halt, withered, waiting for the moving of the water. For an angel went down at a certain season into the pool, and troubled the water: whosoever then first after the troubling of the water stepped in was made whole of whatsoever disease he had. John 5:3-4

> Now four men who were lepers were at the entrance of the city's gate; and they said to one another, *Why do we sit here until we die?* If we say, We will enter the city--then the famine is in the city, and we shall die there; and if we sit still here, we die also... And when these lepers came to the edge of the camp, they went into one tent and ate and drank, and carried away silver, gold, and clothing and went and hid them...2 Kings 7:3-8 (AMP)

As a co-creator with God I came to an understanding that all that was required of me was to do my best. I accepted when I had done all that I could do, God would be the second set of footsteps that would finish the journey for me and give me favor as he did for the lepers. I realized that I did not know what was up ahead of my journey, but I trusted that the provisions would be there when I arrived.

True to his Word, after two years of experiencing unemployment, underemployment, going to night school, and filling out over 400 job applications, I landed a job as a Certified Educator at the age of 57 commensurate with my background and education.

What follows are the inspirational words that encouraged me to *keep moving* during the dark times, the voids in my life. I took to heart the verses below and diligently applied them to my life. Like Jacob I continuously tossed and turned with them through my *mean times*, my night seasons, until they blessed me and became a reality in my life.

> And the earth was without form, and void; and darkness was upon the face of the deep. And the Spirit of God *moved* upon the face of the waters. And God said, *Let there be light: and there was light...* And the evening and the morning were the first day. Genesis 1:2-5

> And God blessed them, and God said unto them, Be fruitful, and multiply, and replenish the earth, and subdue it: and *have dominion* over the fish of the sea, and over the fowl of the air, and over every living thing [*every obstacle, trial, or challenge*] that moves upon the earth. Genesis 1:28.

In regards to health, there is a plethora of scientific studies documenting the health advantages of diet, exercise and nutrition. Articles and research on this subject can be found in any lay or scientific health magazine, book, or journal available in grocery stores, online and in bookstores.

Over 2,000 years later, the hidden wisdom of the scriptures found below in Daniel corroborates what science is now demonstrating through rigorous experiments.

> The king assigned them (the four young men) a daily amount of food and wine from the king's table. They were to be trained for three years, and after that they were to enter the king's service...

> But Daniel resolved not to defile himself with the royal food and wine, and he asked the chief official for permission not to defile himself this way…
>
> Daniel then said to the guard whom the chief official had appointed… "Please test your servants for ten days: *Give us nothing but vegetables to eat and water to drink*. Then compare our appearance with that of the young men who eat the royal food, and treat your servants in accordance with what you see." …
>
> 15 At the *end of the ten days they looked healthier and better nourished than any of the young men who ate the royal food...*
>
> 17 To these four young men God gave knowledge and understanding of all kinds of literature and learning. Daniel 1:5,8,11-13,17, (NIV)

These young men were able to excel in life because they chose healthy foods, worked out, were scholarly, well-read, and spoke with confidence. In essence, they believed that it was important to ***KEEP MOVING*** despite any opposition they encountered in life.

Notes

Step 6:

Pay It Forward & Leave a Legacy

Blessed be the Lord, who daily loads us with benefits....

Psalm 68:19

I praise you because I am fearfully and wonderfully made...

Psalm 139:14 NIV

The psychologist, Abraham Maslow is attributed to saying, "I can feel guilty about the past, apprehensive about the future, but only in the present can I act. The ability to be in the present moment is a major component of mental wellness." Today truly is the only day that we have to act.

According to KidsKonnect.com[36], every day, the human adult has at its command, 100 trillion cells, 206 bones, 600 muscles, and 22 internal organs. Our circulatory system of arteries, veins, and capillaries is about 60,000 miles long. Every hour about 1 billion cells in the human body must be replaced. In an average lifetime, our hearts will beat more than 2.5 billion times. With the strongest muscle in our body, the tongue, we can communicate to others, express ideas, and even win a Grammy for an endearing song.

---

36 *The Human Body*, KidsKonnect. December 1, 2010. http://www.kidskonnect.com/subject-index/31-health/337-human-body.html

Yes, we are fearfully and wonderfully made. With the average brain weighing about 3 pounds we are able to do magnificent things with our bodies, but there is a disclaimer attached to this gift of life. We are only given one day at a time, and between our birth date and death date there is a dash. A period of time for us to actualize who we are, to leave something here on this planet Earth, that hopefully will be a legacy that allows others to enjoy the dashes between their birth and death dates.

This of course begs the question-- what are you doing today with the dash that you have been given? If you have made some mistakes in the past-- get over it, let it go, forgive yourself, and any abuser(s). There is nothing you can do today that can change what happened yesterday. The past is simply the past. As for tomorrow, it's not guaranteed, so don't waste your time worrying about it. We truly don't know whether tomorrow will come.

Look at the two examples below and decide which legacy resembles how you want to spend your dash. Both of these individuals were millionaires. Which one do you think will have a lasting legacy that others will want to emulate?

Living on food stamps

William 'Bud' Post won $16.2 million in the Pennsylvania lottery in 1988 but now lives on his Social Security. 'I wish it never happened. It was totally a nightmare,' says Post.
A former girlfriend successfully sued him for a share of his winnings. It wasn't his only lawsuit. A brother was arrested for hiring a hit man to kill him, hoping to inherit a share of

the winnings. Other siblings pestered him until he agreed to invest in a car business and a restaurant in Sarasota, Fla., -- two ventures that brought no money back and further strained his relationship with his siblings. Post even spent time in jail for firing a gun over the head of a bill collector. Within a year, he was $1 million in debt.

Post admitted he was both careless and foolish, trying to please his family. He eventually declared bankruptcy. Now he lives quietly on $450 a month and food stamps. 'I'm tired, I'm over 65 years old, and I just had a serious operation for a heart aneurysm. Lotteries don't mean (anything) to me,' says Post.[37]

An entrepreneur's grass-roots movement

Millard Fuller became a millionaire before he was 30 by forming a direct-marketing company that sold cookbooks and candy to high school chapters of the Future Homemakers of America. But rather than kick back and enjoy the fruits of his labor, Fuller and his wife, Linda, gave it all away and set out on a life of Christian service that led to the building of homes for more than 1 million people.

The Fullers founded two organizations -- Habitat for Humanity and the Fuller Center for Housing -- that inspire donors to give

---

[37] *8 lottery winners who lost their millions*, msn money. December 1, 2010.

> money, material and labor to build homes for low-income families.[38]

I share these two examples with you because I want you to carefully invest your money, time, and talents as you recover your lost blanket. I hope by now you see that money, your job, a retirement package, or a pension is essentially *an illusion of security.* They only have the appearance of a security blanket. All of these things can be wiped out in an instance--by a crash in the stock market, downsizing, corporation bankruptcy, firm closing, natural disaster, divorce, terminal illness, or other unforeseen events.

My goal is not to scare you; I am not a pessimist. I see myself as a realist and an optimist. As I stated earlier in the book, I see the glass as being half full. The Earth is a magnificent rose garden, but there are thorns in it. I don't see the thorns as a mistake.

Their defensive function allows the rose bush and its fruit to grow, mature, and become hearty. Likewise, the thorns in our life warn us of danger, shape, mold, and mature us. Like a young child that touches a hot stove, we learn to heed a parent's instruction.

Never forget the advice that Billie Holiday gave towards the end of the Great Depression. Her visionary words, "God bless the child that has its own", were prophetic in nature. The individual that has their own, that is, their own self-esteem and the ability to produce from their own loins, from their

---

[38] *Millionaires who gave it away,* msn money. December 1, 2010.

100 trillion cells what they need to thrive in life, is truly blessed.

The only tangible security is *the ability today to manage these cells* in the form of good health, a sound mind, a roof over our head, and friends and family that love us for who we are, and not for how much money or things they can get from us. If you follow the advice that I have given in these 6 Steps and ***KEEP MOVING*** (Step 5), you have my personal guarantee that you will recover your lost income!

My hope is that you will give back to the universe by sharing your wealth--not by giving hand outs, but by providing assistance like micro loans, online crowd funding opportunities, cooperatives, and training--so that individuals can experience a sense of accomplishment that *by their own hands and minds they have created something.* An experience, and a lesson that they can share and pay forward for someone else by being our brother's and sister's keeper on this planet Earth.

Reflection

1. Write what you want your legacy to be. What do you want to be remembered for?

2. Write the names of individuals that have been a blessing in your life. Next, if they are still alive, call or write them and express your gratitude.

3. Whose dreams will you help to make a reality? Who have you been a Good Samaritan to?

4. What have you committed to do today that will improve and expand your life and the lives of others?

Inspirational Nuggets

John Donne coined the phrase, "No man is an island to himself; every man is a piece of the continent." Time has taught me that our successes and failures in life are not ours alone. They come about from individuals and groups working hand and hand to improve or diminish man's lot in life. Scientific studies have shown that the over consumption of the world resources by developed countries can adversely affect not only the environments in third world countries, but also those in developed countries. Likewise, how we treat one another on an interpersonal level, affects all of us.

Although my beginnings were humble and lacking in many ways, I have been blessed to rise above poverty, family discord, dysfunction, emotional abuse, unemployment and underemployment. Consequently, I feel compelled to share with others how they can not only overcome this present day economic recession, but any economic challenge in the future.

In my daily walk, I try to personify a quote of Dr. Martin Luther King Jr., in which he stated the following: "An individual has not started living until he can rise above the narrow confines of his individualistic concerns to the broader concerns of all humanity."

The following two allegories impressed on me that we are interconnected on this planet Earth. Although we are separated by languages and continents, ultimately we are responsible for our brother's successes and failures.

> And Cain talked with Abel his brother: and it came to pass, when they were in the field, that Cain rose up against Abel his brother, and slew him.
>
> And the LORD said unto Cain, Where is Abel thy brother? And he said, I know not: *Am I my brother's keeper?*
>
> And he said, *What hast thou done?* the voice of thy brother's blood crieth unto me from the ground. Genesis 4:8-10

> Looking for a loophole, he asked, "*And just how would you define 'neighbor'?*" Jesus answered by telling a story. "There was once a man traveling from Jerusalem to Jericho. On the way he was attacked by robbers. They took his clothes, beat him up, and went off leaving him half-dead. Luckily, a priest was on his way down the same road, but when he saw him he angled across to the other side. Then a Levite religious man showed up; he also avoided the injured man.
>
> "A Samaritan traveling the road came on him. When he saw the man's condition, his heart

> went out to him. He gave him first aid, disinfecting and bandaging his wounds. Then he lifted him onto his donkey, led him to an inn, and made him comfortable. In the morning he took out two silver coins and gave them to the innkeeper, saying, '*Take good care of him. If it costs any more, put it on my bill—I'll pay you on my way back.*' What do you think? Which of the three became a neighbor to the man attacked by robbers? 'The one who treated him kindly,' the religion scholar responded. Jesus said, 'Go and do the same'" Luke 10:29-37 (MSG).

I shared with you earlier in the Acknowledgement section, how I was challenged by the words of President John F. Kennedy to be an asset and not a liability as an American citizen. His words still ring out loudly today in the 21st century. They beckon for citizens of the world to be Good Samaritans. Brother's keepers who will influence the world by using their witty inventions, gifts, and talents in order to offer solutions that will alleviate poverty, illness, diseases, and world hunger.

Native Americans believe strongly in leaving a legacy and being their brother's keeper. Chief Maquinna, a Nootka Native American, did not worry about who stole his blanket, his sense of security. As one of their leaders he explained their commitment to humanity as follows: "Once I was in Victoria, and I saw a very large house. They told me it was a bank and that the white men place their money there to be taken care of, and that by and by they got it back with interest. We are Indians and we have no such bank; but when we have plenty of money or *blankets, we give them away* to other chiefs and people, and by and by *they return them with interest, and our hearts feel good. Our way of giving is our bank."*

Now is the time to ask yourself-- what footprint are you leaving for eternity? Who have you given a blanket to? What will your dash reveal about how you spent the gift of life? As you follow these steps I have outlined in this book, and climb your ladder of economic success, always remember to reach back and empower someone else to fulfill their dreams!

RESOURCES

[Note to the reader: Detailed below are national resources which offer aid to individuals seeking education, employment, housing, and health assistance. This list is by no means exhaustive, but is an attempt to identify resources found in most major cities or online across the United States. The author is not affiliated with and does not personally endorse any of these organizations, and is not responsible or liable for any of their services or products.]

- http://www.literacydirectory.org
- http://www.direct.ed.gov (Federal Student Aid)
- http://www.employmentguide.com/
- www.snagajob.com
- http://www.careeronestop.org
- www.jobfox.com
- www.getthejob.com
- www.careerbuilder.com
- http://www.kickstarter.com (funding platform for creative projects)
- http://www.dol.gov (U. S. Dept of Labor)
- http://www.womenshealth.gov (National Women's Health Information Center)
- http://debtorsanonymous.org (Debtors Anonymous)
- www.hud.gov (U.S. Department of Housing and Urban Development)

Notes

ABOUT THE AUTHOR

C. JOYCE FARRAR-ROSEMON, BA, SM, Ed.S., never envisioned as she sat on the inner city housing projects steps in Boston that she would become a successful businesswoman who would one day earn a six figure income and go on to become a highly acclaimed Motivational Speaker. In 1992, Joyce married and opened a real estate company in her seventh month of pregnancy with only $10.00 in the operating account. That investment subsequently blossomed into a six-figure income.

Joyce has not only survived, but has thrived after living in a dysfunctional family. She has overcome poverty, abuse, loneliness, depression, job loss, a stillbirth and two miscarriages. Joyce has gone from making six figures – to no figures. Following the collapse of the real estate industry in 2007, Joyce experienced unemployment and worked several low paying jobs for two years. During that time, she returned to school – and after filling out close to 400 applications, Joyce eventually landed a job as a Certified Educator at the age of 57.

Farrar-Rosemon speaks frequently to nonprofit groups, schools, colleges and churches. She has appeared in several newspapers, magazines, on radio and television, including The Geraldo at Large Show. She is now a best-selling author, Certified Educator, Radio Host of *Inspirational Voices,* and holds a bachelor's degree in psychology and elementary education and a master's in psychiatric social work from Simmons College in Boston, Massachusetts. Joyce earned her Specialist Degree in Education from Mercer University in the fall of 2012. She and her husband, Tillmon H. Rosemon Jr., live in Atlanta, Georgia. They have one son, David.

For information on how to book Joyce for speaking engagements, or Empowerment Seminars, click on www.womensempowermentseminars.com or email Joyce at joycerosemon@gmail.com.

BIBLIOGRAPHY

Farrar-Rosemon, C. Joyce. *How to Be the HEAD and NOT the TAIL! A Christian Manifesto for Making Six Figures*. Franklin, Tenn., Providence House Publishers, 2005.

Farrar-Rosemon, C. Joyce. *How to Get To The Palace From Your Prison! Joseph's 14 Step Program To Overcome Loneliness, Depression, discrimination, Barrenness & Abuse.* Atlanta, GA., Winner At Life Publishers, 2013.

Gardner, Chris. *The Pursuit Of Happyness,* New York: Amistad, 2006.

Sullivan, Otha Richard. *African American Women Scientists and Inventors.* (New York: Wiley, 2002), 27.

PUBLICATIONS

This book marks the third in a series of "*how to*" books by Joyce. Her first, *How to Be the HEAD and NOT the TAIL!: A Christian Manifesto for Making Six Figures* details how Joyce relied on biblical truths and business principles to become a multi-million dollar producer in the real estate arena.

Her second book, *HOW to GET to THE PALACE from YOUR PRISON* continues along the lines of the first by giving readers practical "how to steps" to achieve one's goals in life. *HOW to GET to THE PALACE's* emphasis is on overcoming the emotional and psychological problems that prevent individuals from achieving a sense of shalom [nothing missing and nothing broken], regardless of their background, race, gender, or birthplace. For information on obtaining these books, go to www.womensempowermentseminars.com or email Joyce at joycerosemon@gmail.com.

Made in the USA
Charleston, SC
21 August 2013